Helping Your Children with Change

Holding Fast to God During Upheaval

Darby A. Strickland

New Growth Press, Greensboro, NC 27401
newgrowthpress.com
Copyright © 2025 by Darby A. Strickland

All rights reserved. No part of this publication may be reproduced, stored in a retrieval system, or transmitted in any form by any means, electronic, mechanical, photocopy, recording, or otherwise, without the prior permission of the publisher, except as provided by USA copyright law.

Unless otherwise noted, Scripture quotations are taken from The ESV® Bible (The Holy Bible, English Standard Version®). ESV® Text Edition: 2016. Copyright © 2001 by Crossway, a publishing ministry of Good News Publishers. The ESV® text has been reproduced in cooperation with and by permission of Good News Publishers. Unauthorized reproduction of this publication is prohibited. All rights reserved.

Scripture verses marked ICB are taken from The Holy Bible, International Children's Bible® Copyright © 1986, 1988, 1999, 2015 by Thomas Nelson. Used by permission.

Cover Design: Dan Stelzer
Interior Typesetting and Ebook: Lisa Parnell,
lparnellbookservices.com

ISBN: 978-1-64507-530-1 (print)
ISBN: 978-1-64507-531-8 (ebook)

Library of Congress Cataloging-in-Publication Data on file

Printed in India

29 28 27 26 25   1 2 3 4 5

Embracing Change Together

Change is hard for all of us, but for children, it can feel especially overwhelming. As parents, you are uniquely placed to walk alongside your children as guides. You show them the steady, compassionate care of their heavenly Father. It is not about having all the answers or fixing everything for them—it's about being present, offering your love and stability, and pointing them to the God whose love never wavers.

Meanwhile, don't forget your own needs. As a parent, you feel the constant pull to prioritize your children, but one way to care for your children is to care for yourself. Seek healing for your hurts, fears, and confusion so that you can freely shepherd your children through their own emotions and concerns. Lean on Jesus and other adults for care and strength. It will bless your children to witness God's restorative work in your life through your trust in his faithfulness.

Since change can be unsettling for you, too, this is also a time to depend on God more fully. As you rely on his strength, your children will see that dependence, and it will speak to them of his sufficiency and tender care when we are overwhelmed. With your love, patience, and God's unshakable care, your children can begin to see that they are never alone in life's changes. Instead, they are fully known, deeply loved, and held by the One who never changes. These moments, while difficult, are sacred opportunities for your children to grow in their trust in him—and for you to grow alongside them.

You will all experience complex emotions. Encourage your children to express theirs by talking, drawing, or journaling. Children may not tell you everything they feel; they might be afraid to hurt you or add to your pain. So remind them that God fully knows their hearts and feelings. Divorce brings many losses: Grieving is vital. Provide space for your children to express sorrow—maybe even lament with them—helping them talk to God about what hurts and worries them.

Children will want to know how divorce will impact them. They need you to talk about their needs. So, center your interactions on their needs and concerns. Children are practical; they'll want to know where they will live and go to school and what their new room will look like. If you and their other parent can provide those answers, it will bless your children and reassure them that you have considered their concerns. Collaborating with their other parent to maintain consistent routines will offer the stability children crave.

If details are uncertain, be honest with your children. Say something like, "We're still working on figuring things out, but we'll let you know as soon as we can." If the situation is contentious, you might say, "We're having trouble working these things out, but other adults are helping us, and I trust that God knows exactly what we need." Constantly reassure your children that their concerns matter to you and the Lord, who has promised to provide.

that even in a brand-new classroom, God is always beside them to provide comfort and strength.

To help your children prepare:

1. Consider visiting the school together or meeting their teacher beforehand, creating a sense of familiarity before the first day.
2. Take time to pray with them, asking God to fill their hearts with courage and peace as they begin this new journey.
3. Engage in role-playing activities to practice introductions and classroom scenarios, building their confidence and easing their nerves.

These small preparations can make a big difference in helping them feel secure and ready.

Encourage your children to rely on God's strength as they navigate new social situations, reminding them that even their smallest steps of courage reflect God's faithfulness. Celebrate their successes together, helping them see how God is guiding their path and helping them grow. While this transition may feel challenging, it's also a precious opportunity for their faith to deepen as they experience God's loving provision and care.

Adjusting to Divorce or Separation

Divorce or separation can be confusing and painful for children, but it also offers an opportunity to anchor them in God's unchanging love. Psalm 136:1 tells us that God's "steadfast love endures forever." Reassure your children that while life may feel uncertain, God's love and care is constant and unwavering.

they live, God is their eternal home and will always be with them.

To help them feel more secure, involve them in the process—let them help pack their favorite belongings, choose how to set up their new room, or pick an exciting spot to visit in the new neighborhood. This gives them a sense of agency and participation in an overwhelming time. Practically, you can prepare them for the transition by helping them say goodbye to the people and places they love, affirming the relationships they've built. As you do, reassure them that just as God provided for them here, he will care for them in their new home, gifting new friendships and joys.

Take time to pray together for their new home and neighborhood, asking God to bless this fresh start. Once you've moved, establish familiar routines, like bedtime prayers or family meals, to create a sense of continuity. These practices can help your children feel grounded in their new environment; they will help them feel safe, secure, and loved, knowing God will provide what they need.

Acclimating to a New School

Starting a new school can feel daunting for children, but it's also a meaningful opportunity to remind them of God's promise in Deuteronomy 31:6: "Be strong and courageous. Do not fear or be in dread of them, for it is the LORD your God who goes with you. He will not leave you or forsake you." Reassure your children

- *Provide small choices.* Involve children in decisions to give them a sense of agency (e.g., picking a favorite toy to bring to a new home or school).
- *Create familiarity.* Carry comforting items like a stuffed animal, blanket, or family photo into new settings.
- *Create.* Write promises like Psalm 139:10 ("Your right hand shall hold me") on a bookmark or draw a picture of what it feels like to be held by God. Use a jar to collect their worries through prayer, symbolizing giving their fears to God.
- *Role-play scenarios.* Practice new situations together (e.g., meeting new people at school or exploring a new home).
- *Rejoice in God's provision.* Share stories of how God has cared for your family in the past to build trust in his faithfulness.
- *Verbalize your dependence on God.* Let your children see that you trust God's guidance and care in your life.

With these general principles in mind, let's now focus on specific occasions for change, their unique challenges for children, and ways you can guide them.

Moving to a New Home

Moving to a new home can be unsettling for children. Remind them of the truth that God is with them no matter where they go (Psalm 139:7). God is our ultimate dwelling place (Psalm 90:1); no matter where

Tangible Ways to Comfort Children Amidst Change

Here are some methods for comforting your children when they are anxious about change. We will first look at comforts that apply more generally and then explore the most common types of change, offering specific ways to address them.

- *Be consistent.* During change, maintain bedtime prayers, family meals, or other familiar routines. Demonstrate stability by following through on commitments, no matter how small.
- *Read "A Big Change Happened."* Follow Wallace the Whale's migration as the truths of Psalm 139 come to life in this companion picture book.
- *Create a God-centered routine.* Encourage daily moments of reflection, such as reading a short psalm or thanking God for small blessings, to emphasize God's constancy. Start and end the day with prayer for help to trust in his plan.
- *Listen to their worries.* Invite children to share their hearts without dismissing or rushing them.
- *Identify their emotions.* Help children identify and express their feelings. Assure them it's normal to feel unsure about change, but God equips them to face it.
- *Listen to worship music.* Shane and Shane have a song for children called "You Know Everything," based on Psalm 139.

show them they are not alone. When your children experience difficult emotions, meet them with heart-centered truths. For fear, remind them, "God's hand will hold you fast" (Psalm 139:10). For sadness, reassure them, "God knows your every thought and cares for you" (v. 2). For loneliness, affirm, "You are never alone; God is always with you" (vv. 7–10). Encourage them to pray about their anger or confusion, knowing that God understands their every thought (v. 4).

Use simple and honest explanations to help your children make sense of the change without overwhelming them. For instance, if you're moving, you could say, "We're moving to a new home where you'll have your own room." For divorce, you might explain, "Mom and Dad will live in different houses, but we both love you very much." If they're starting a new school, share, "You'll meet new friends and learn fun things at your new school." These clear, straightforward explanations provide comfort and clarity amid uncertainty.

Above all, continue to affirm your love and provide reassurance of their security within your family. Repeat messages of stability, like, "We will get through this together," or "No matter what changes, my love for you will never change." Help them trust in God's constant care and presence, alongside the steady love of their family. These reassurances, paired with your consistent support, will help your children feel more secure and grounded as they adjust to new circumstances.

How can we practically model this truth in our parenting? In the next section, we'll explore practical tools and biblical wisdom to help you support your children during times of change.

Helping Your Children Understand and Navigate Change

Having reflected on the profound truths of Psalm 139, let's consider how to live them out as we parent our children. This is no easy task, especially during life's challenges and uncertainties. Even so, it is a deeply hopeful calling. Our children learn about who God is and how he loves them when we intentionally model his heart in our parenting. In this section, we'll explore how we can showcase the aspects of God's character—his desire to know them intimately, his steadfast love, and his unwavering presence—that we want our children to see, trust, and count on amid life's changes. Despite our imperfections, we have the privilege of pointing our children to the perfect Shepherd who knows and loves them completely.

The first step is to slow down and understand what your child is feeling. What are they anxious about? What losses are they mourning?

When children face change, it's vital to create a safe space where they feel comfortable asking questions and expressing their emotions. Let them know it's okay to feel scared, sad, confused, or even excited. By patiently listening and validating their feelings, you also forms our days, shaping them into a story of grace that glorifies him.

Share this truth with your children: Even before you were born, God planned every one of your days (Psalm 139:16). He knew about the happy times you would celebrate and the hard times you would face. When you don't understand why something is happening, you can trust that God knows your whole story. And when you have lots of questions, you can share them with me, and we can talk to God about them together.

The best part is that God doesn't just write your story—he walks through it with you. He goes before you to guide you, follows behind and protects you, and holds your hand every step of the way (v. 5). You can rest in the comforting truth that the God who made you and loves you is shaping your story into something that brings him glory and is for your good. You are never alone, and your story is always in his hands.

> Key Verse: "You saw my body as it was formed. All the days planned for me were written in your book before I was one day old." (Psalm 139:16 ICB)

Psalm 139 reveals a God who intimately knows, surrounds, and shapes his people with unfailing love and sovereign care. These truths not only provide peace for our own hearts but offer a foundation of comfort and security we can share with our children as they navigate the uncertainties of life. The question remains:

God shapes his people's stories

Psalm 139 reveals the wondrous truth that the stories of God's people are not the result of chance or chaos but are lovingly crafted by his sovereign hand. David declares, "Your eyes saw my unformed substance; in your book were written, every one of them, the days that were formed for me, when as yet there was none of them" (v. 16). Before we took our first breath, God had already penned the narrative of our lives. Each chapter, filled with both joy and struggle, is written by a God who is infinitely wise and unfailingly good.

God's shaping of our stories does not mean we won't face difficulty or sorrow, but it does mean that every moment is purposeful. God weaves together the joys and the trials, the triumphs and the tears, into a tapestry that reflects his glory and fulfills his eternal purposes. David's exclamation, "Such knowledge is too wonderful for me; it is high; I cannot attain it" (v. 6), reminds us that while we may not understand our story as it unfolds, we can trust that the author of our days knows the ending, and it is good.

In his intimate care, God not only shapes our individual stories but also weaves them into the grand story of redemption. Our days are not isolated fragments but threads in the larger fabric of his kingdom purposes. We can entrust our story to Jesus, the author and perfecter of our faith (Hebrews 12:2). In every season, we can find peace knowing that the God who formed us

His love pierces through our fears, offering both light and direction.

To be surrounded by God means to dwell in a reality that transcends life's uncertainties. His presence is a refuge and resting place for weary souls. He goes behind and before, above and beneath, encircling us with his loving, sovereign care. God is intimately near, watching over us with the love and care of a devoted shepherd. What greater reassurance could we have than knowing we are never alone, no matter where life takes us?

Share this truth with your children: I want you to remember something very special—God is always with you, no matter where you go. The Bible says, "You are all around me—in front and in back. You have put your hand on me." (Psalm 139:5 ICB). That means that wherever you are, God's love surrounds you completely, like a big, loving hug that never ends. Even when things feel a little scary or uncertain, you can trust that God is right there with you. The Bible reminds us that even the darkest night isn't dark to God—his love shines brighter than any shadow (vv. 11–12). His presence is like a strong fortress, protecting you and giving you a place to feel safe, loved, and cared for every moment of your life. You're never alone, and you're always held by his unchanging love.

> Key Verse: "You are all around me—in front and in back. You have put your hand on me." (Psalm 139:5 ICB)

knows when you wake up and when you go to bed. Nothing escapes him.

God is your loving heavenly Father who watches over you every moment, every day. He knows exactly what you need and understands what you're afraid of. When you feel happy, sad, afraid, or even mad, he sees it all and is ready to help. You can trust that you are always seen, always known, and always loved by him, no matter what.

> Key Verse: "You know when I sit down and when I get up. You know my thoughts before I think them." (Psalm 139:2 ICB)

God surrounds his people with his presence

Psalm 139 presents a comforting vision of God who envelops his people in tender protection (v. 5). God's presence is not an abstract force, but the intentional and compassionate care of our Creator, who understands our frailty and shields us from harm.

God's nearness knows no boundaries. David poignantly asks, "Where shall I go from your Spirit? Or where shall I flee from your presence?" (v. 7). The answer is both comforting and clear: There is nowhere beyond God's reach. Whether we are soaring in joy or sinking in despair, his hand is always there to guide and support us (vv. 8–10). In our darkest moments, when fear and uncertainty cloud our vision, God's closeness remains unwavering: "Even the darkness is not dark to you; the night is bright as the day" (v. 12).

have searched me and known me" (v. 1). The word "searched" implies a thorough and heartfelt examination. God knows our actions and the very thoughts that precede them. Before we even speak a word, he understands what is on our hearts (v. 4).

God's knowledge is personal, relational, and deeply compassionate. He knows when we sit and when we get up (v. 2). Such understanding might initially unsettle us, but his tender care should temper our fear. God's sight is neither detached nor condemning; it is protective and filled with purpose. He sees us in our vulnerability, our mistakes, and our moments of despair, yet he never withdraws. He stays close. His gaze penetrates the shadows that obscure our understanding, assuring us that his sustaining love defies any darkness we may face.

How comforting it is to know that God sees not just the surface, but the depths of who we are? He has searched and known us, and he still loves us. Just as we watch over our children to protect and guide them, God watches over us in his fatherly love. His sight is a constant, unwavering expression of his commitment. Each day unfolds under the steady gaze of a God who fully sees and perfectly loves us. This assurance forms the foundation of our confidence: We are never unseen, never unknown, and never unloved.

Share this truth with your children: God sees you perfectly at all times because he loves you. He knows everything about you—your thoughts, your feelings, and what you might say even before you say it. He

Wonderful are your works;
   my soul knows it very well.
My frame was not hidden from you,
when I was being made in secret,
   intricately woven in the depths of the earth.
Your eyes saw my unformed substance;
in your book were written, every one of them,
   the days that were formed for me,
   when as yet there was none of them.
   (Psalm 139:1–16)

David wrote Psalm 139 as a profound reflection on the God who sees, surrounds, and shapes the stories of his people. In it, David expresses deep awareness of God's intimate involvement in every aspect of his life, finding great comfort in the inescapable and personal presence of the Lord. He marvels at the vastness of God's power and presence while being reassured by the tender care of the God who lays his hand upon his people and holds them fast (v. 5, 10). His hand upon us signifies that he is near, actively involved in our lives, and attentive to our needs. It reminds us that we are never out of his reach or care. His hand steadies us even when life feels uncertain or overwhelming.

God has perfect sight of his people

Psalm 139 invites us to marvel at the intimate, unfailing sight of God upon his people. God sees us not with a fleeting glance or an impersonal observation, but with the deep, searching gaze of our Creator who knows us entirely. David begins, "O Lord, you are graciously guided, even when life feels confusing or uncertain.

> O Lord, you have searched me and known me!
> You know when I sit down and when I rise up;
> > you discern my thoughts from afar.
> You search out my path and my lying down
> > and are acquainted with all my ways.
> Even before a word is on my tongue,
> > behold, O Lord, you know it altogether.
> You hem me in, behind and before,
> > and lay your hand upon me.
> Such knowledge is too wonderful for me;
> > it is high; I cannot attain it.
> Where shall I go from your Spirit?
> > Or where shall I flee from your presence?
> If I ascend to heaven, you are there!
> > If I make my bed in Sheol, you are there!
> If I take the wings of the morning
> > and dwell in the uttermost parts of the sea,
> even there your hand shall lead me,
> > and your right hand shall hold me.
> If I say, "Surely the darkness shall cover me,
> > and the light about me be night,"
> even the darkness is not dark to you;
> > the night is bright as the day,
> > for darkness is as light with you.
> For you formed my inward parts;
> > you knitted me together in my mother's womb.
> I praise you, for I am fearfully and wonderfully made.

children navigate challenges, promote healing, and foster healthy adjustment to the changes they face.

We must remember that a child's response to change flows from their heart, which, according to Scripture, is the control center of their thoughts, emotions, and desires. In seasons of transition, their reactions—whether anxiety, resistance, or sadness—reveal deeper heart struggles shaped by fears, longings for security, and, of course, trying to manage life without God's help. Ultimately, they need to be reminded of God's promise: "Fear not, for I am with you" (Isaiah 41:10), as they learn to trust in his nearness even when their small world feels uncertain.

It is normal for children to fear losing connections or their sense of belonging. These are opportunities to guide them to lean on God, whose word guides us, "When I am afraid, I put my trust in you" (Psalm 56:3). By shepherding their hearts with compassion and Scripture, parents can point their children to the faithfulness of God, even amidst life's uncertainties.

Psalm 139 and the Hand of God

Psalm 139 is a wonderful passage of Scripture to use to give your children reassuring truths about who the Lord is and how he will be with them through every change. As you read the first sixteen verses, notice how Psalm 139 draws us into the wonder of God's care. God knows our thoughts, our steps, our fears, and even our unspoken words. David reminds us that we

- Excessive clinginess: reluctance to separate from parents or caregivers or seeking constant reassurance.
- Persistent questions: asking repetitive questions about the change, even after receiving answers.
- Behavioral regression: for instance, thumb-sucking, bedwetting, or using baby talk.
- Withdrawal: avoiding interactions with friends or family, preferring isolation, and loss of interest in toys, games, or hobbies they usually enjoy.
- Hyperactivity: becoming unusually fidgety, restless, or unable to focus on tasks.
- Sleep disturbances: difficulty falling or staying asleep, and nightmares.
- Physical complaints: headaches, stomachaches, or other unexplained ailments that might be stress related.
- Difficulty concentrating: trouble focusing on schoolwork or activities they previously enjoyed.
- Forgetfulness: more frequent inattentiveness regarding tasks or instructions than usual.

Responses to the stress of change can significantly disrupt children's daily life and emotional well-being. While some children may show only short-term reactions, others may experience longer-lasting effects that require attention. If these behaviors persist for a few months or worsen, seek guidance from a counselor or pediatrician. Their expertise, combined with your care and support, can provide valuable tools to help your feeling. Their seemingly defiant behavior is really their way of saying, "I feel scared or confused."

Change affects children in elementary school (ages six through eleven) differently. They're beginning to grasp cause-and-effect relationships and have a broader social world, which means they are processing transitions on multiple levels. They may express their worries more directly, often through repeated questions about what to expect or by sharing sadness over what they're losing, like friends or familiar routines. Their feelings might also come through in actions—expressing anger, withdrawing socially, or acting out in ways you haven't seen before. Since friends and social connections are increasingly important at this age, changes that impact those relationships—like a new school or neighborhood—can feel particularly destabilizing. While they can articulate more than younger children, they still need help naming and making sense of what they're feeling.

Here's a list of signs that children (ages two to eleven) *might* be overwhelmed by change. These reactions often signal that a transition is causing significant stress:

- Increased anxiety: worrying, fearfulness, or preoccupation with "what if" scenarios.
- Sadness or hopelessness: tearfulness, feelings of helplessness, or expressing thoughts like, "Everything is ruined."
- Anger or irritability: uncharacteristic frustration, lashing out at family members, showing defiance, or testing boundaries more than usual.

and sovereign control for good remain anchors, even in life's most difficult transitions. Whether your children are facing a move, starting a new school, or adjusting to a new family dynamic, you can point them to the steadfast care of the One who knows them intimately, surrounds them, and lovingly shapes their story. With God's guidance and your intentional care, your children can learn to face change with faith and confidence, resting in the truth that they are fully known, deeply loved, and never alone.

How Children React to Change

When young children (particularly preschoolers aged two to five) encounter change, they can feel disoriented because they rely so heavily on routines to make sense of their world. They thrive on predictability—it helps them feel safe and secure. So, when their world shifts unexpectedly, whether because of a move, the arrival of a new sibling, or another change in family dynamics, they may struggle to process it verbally. You might already have noticed this when minor disruptions, like a missed favorite show, cause an outsized reaction. With more significant changes, young children may revert to earlier developmental behaviors they had previously outgrown, such as thumb-sucking, clinginess, or trouble sleeping, as they seek comfort in something familiar. It's not uncommon for them to act out through tantrums or by exhibiting heightened anxiety because they still lack the words to explain what they're

How do I keep this from breaking them?" she blurted out before she even sat down. Sarah's questions were painful, and they came from her deep love for her children and the weight of her responsibility as their mother. Instinctively, she knew she could do nothing to negate the fact that the changes ahead would be painful for everyone.

As parents, our children's well-being is of utmost importance to us. So, when we see them struggling with change, we feel burdened. Sometimes, the upheaval they are enduring is equally difficult for us. When we have fears about what's next, it can be harder to offer children reassurance. The changes they face often stem from decisions we make or circumstances we are mourning, which can add guilt to the mix. In these moments, it's crucial to remember that we don't need to have all the answers or carry these burdens alone. God invites us to bring our fears, guilt, and grief to him, trusting that his love is sufficient for us and our children. As we rely on his help to navigate these challenges, we can point our children to the same unchanging source of hope, showing them that even in the hardest transitions, we are held by the one who never changes.

This minibook explores the challenges children face during times of upheaval and how we, as parents, can address these challenges and our own. It will provide biblical truths and practical tools to help you support your children when they encounter the challenges that accompany change. Drawing deeply from Psalm 139 will remind us that God's love, presence, or even frightening to them. That's why we must guide them through life's transitions with patience, understanding, and steady reassurance. They need to know they're not alone and that we'll be there to help them find their footing in the unfamiliar.

When I first met Liam in my counseling office, he sat quietly on the edge of his chair, his small hands gripping the seat as if it might suddenly tip over. His mom explained that their family was preparing to move to a new town in two months, and ever since he found out, Liam had been unusually quiet and withdrawn. He often cried at bedtime and clung to his mom whenever she tried to discuss the move. "He's just so scared," she said, her voice heavy with concern.

I asked Liam to tell me why the move seemed hard. After a pause, he said, "What if I don't make any friends? What if our new house isn't as nice? What if it doesn't feel like home?" I reassured Liam that these were good questions. Moving is hard for everyone, but for a seven-year-old, it can feel as if their entire world is being uprooted.

While we as parents have the emotional resources to manage transitions for ourselves, we often struggle when we witness our children struggling. I've seen many parents suffer when anticipating the impact of change upon their children. For example, when Sarah walked into my office, she looked exhausted. Her hands nervously twisted the strap of her bag, "I just don't know how they're going to handle it. My kids—they're everything to me. This divorce is going to shatter them.

Change is part of life. I'm writing this on a beautiful fall day, and I delight in noticing that the leaves' colors have turned golden yellow and fiery red in the cooling air. But I am less excited about the coming change to bitter cold and leafless trees. My mixed emotions reflect how we feel about most changes. Some changes cause excitement, like a new baby or a better job. But we dread difficult changes, like divorce, an unwelcome move, or downsizing due to financial hardship.

Even positive changes can carry a subtle sadness, a sense of loss for what was. Recently, our family moved into a wonderful new home, but this also meant finding a new church. Walking into a room of unfamiliar faces, I was met with kind smiles and warm greetings. Yet, instead of being comforted, I felt overwhelmed. My heart ached for my old friends and the deep sense of being known and loved by my previous church family. In those early days, I couldn't help but long for the familiar warmth of what had been my church home.

How Children Experience Change

As adults, we can hold conflicting emotions and remind ourselves that these feelings won't last forever. In time, this new space will feel familiar, too. But for children, change can be even more unsettling. Their limited experience makes it difficult for them to process uncertainty. Plus, they are still learning how the world works and how to process big feelings. What we, as adults, can reason through might feel overwhelming